Things with Wings

Written by Carson Creagh

TIME
LIFE
BOOKS

**The Nature Company Young Discoveries Library
is published by Time-Life Books.**

Conceived and produced by
Weldon Owen Pty Limited
43 Victoria Street, McMahons Point,
NSW, 2060, Australia
A member of the
Weldon Owen Group of Companies
Sydney • San Francisco
Copyright 1996 © US Weldon Owen Inc.
Copyright 1996 © Weldon Owen Pty Limited

THE NATURE COMPANY
Priscilla Wrubel, Ed Strobin, Steve Manning,
Georganne Papac, Tracy Fortini

TIME-LIFE BOOKS
Time-Life Books is a division of Time Life Inc.
Time-Life is a trademark of Time Warner Inc. U.S.A.

Vice President and Publisher: Terry Newell
Editorial Director: Donia A. Steele
Director of New Product Development: Regina Hall
Director of Sales: Neil Levin
Director of Financial Operations: J. Brian Birky

WELDON OWEN Pty Limited
President: John Owen
Publisher: Sheena Coupe
Managing Editor: Rosemary McDonald
Project Editor: Jenni Bruce
Text Editor: Claire Craig
Art Director: Sue Burk
Designer: Robyn Latimer
Picture Research: Libby Frederico
Production Manager: Caroline Webber
Vice President, International Sales: Stuart Laurence
Coeditions Director: Derek Barton
Subject Consultants: Daniel Bickel, Dr. David Kirshner,
Terence Lindsey, Dr. George McKay, Dr. Paul Willis

Library of Congress
Cataloging-in-Publication Data
Things with wings / Carson Creagh.
    p. cm. -- (Young discoveries)

    ISBN 0-7835-4838-9

    1. Animals--Juvenile literature. 2. Animal
flight--Juvenile literature. [1. Animals. 2. Animal
flight. 3. Wings.] I. Title. II. Series.
QL49.C725   1996
591--dc20   96-15736

Manufactured by Mandarin Offset
Printed in China

A Weldon Owen Production

Contents

What Things Can Fly?

▲ A bird curves its wings to push against the air.

Birds, bats, and insects are the only animals that can truly fly. They all flap their wings to "push" themselves through the air. Insects such as bees, dragonflies, beetles, butterflies, and grasshoppers are the smallest flying animals. They have four wings, while bats and birds have only two. Bats' wings are made of skin. Birds' wings are covered with hundreds of feathers. Even penguins, which "fly" underwater, have feathers on their wings.

◄ A bat's wings stretch from its long fingers to its hind legs.

4

How many wings does a dragonfly have?

▼ Dragonflies can flap their wings up to 50 times a second.

◀ Dragonflies first appeared more than 300 million years ago. Some of the early dragonflies had a wingspan of almost three feet.

5

Ladybugs

Ladybugs are beetles. They fly from plant to plant hunting insects called aphids. Most ladybugs are red or yellow and have black spots. The bright colors warn birds that they are poisonous. If attacked, a ladybug will play dead by rolling over on its back and squirting out a smelly yellow juice. Ladybugs sleep through winter because there are no aphids to eat. In very cold places, thousands of ladybugs hide beneath the snow, huddling together to stay warm until spring.

◀Aphids eat plants, so ladybugs, which eat aphids, are welcome in the garden.

▲ Ladybugs have hard, spotted wing cases. These protect a ladybug's real wings, which fold up beneath the wing cases when it lands.

▶ Ladybugs are sometimes named after the number of spots on their wing cases. The five-spot ladybug and the ten-spot ladybug are shown here.

Some ladybugs have stripes instead of spots on their wing cases.

Wings and Stings

▶ Wasps and bees taste and smell with their antennae.

Wasps and bees are flying insects. They have delicate, see-through wings to carry them far and wide in search of food. Bees sip sweet nectar and gather pollen from flowers. They make the nectar into honey for their young. Wasps hunt for their food, which is usually other insects. Wasps and bees have stingers to help protect them from attackers. Their yellow and black markings warn hungry enemies to stay away, or they might end up with a nasty sting instead of a tasty meal.

Can you spot the bulging bags of yellow pollen on the legs of the honeybees?

Wasps' wings beat to

make a buzzing sound

► Honeybees live in a special home called a hive. They make honey to feed the baby bees that grow inside the honeycomb chambers of the hive.

▼ Inside the wasp there is a sac of poison and a needlelike stinger.

▼ Sometimes honeybees fly in large groups called swarms.

Butterfly Flutters

Butterflies flutter from flower to flower, drinking sweet nectar. Many butterflies are brightly colored to warn predators that they taste bad. Some have bright colors on top of their wings and dull colors underneath. When they land and fold their wings, they seem to disappear. Most butterflies fly during the day, while their relatives, the moths, take over at night. The yellow emperor moth has eye-shaped spots on its wings that fool its enemies into thinking it is much bigger than it really is.

► A butterfly's beautiful colors tell other butterflies what kind it is, and warn its enemies to stay away.

A butterfly

◄ When a butterfly is resting, it holds its wings up behind its back.

◄ When a moth is resting, its wings lie flat.

10

has

four wings

▲ The bright colors on
a butterfly's wings are
made up of thousands
of tiny scales.

*Some butterflies
fly thousands of
miles to a warmer
place when winter
approaches.*

11

Dancing Wings

Fireflies are beetles that fly at night. They never lose each other in the dark because they have bright lights in their tails and can flash messages. There are many different kinds of fireflies. When looking for mates, male and female fireflies flash special codes to each other to make sure they attract their own kind. Some female fireflies cheat and flash another firefly's code to attract a male. When the male lands, the female eats him.

A firefly's eggs and babies also glow in the dark.

▶ Male fireflies fly close to the ground. Each kind performs a special dance, flashing its light in a different pattern.

◀ Female fireflies do not fly. They sit on the ground, flashing their lights to attract mates.

In a Flap

A bird's body is like a flying machine. A hummingbird can hover, a peregrine falcon can dive at 170 miles per hour, and a wandering albatross can fly for a month without landing. Birds are covered with light, strong feathers. Their bones have bubbles of air inside them and are also light and strong. Because birds are not very heavy, they do not have to use a lot of energy to stay in the air. Even their muscles can work for a long time without getting tired and sore.

▲ Swallows and swifts catch mosquitoes and midges while flying. They can even take a short nap in the air.

▶ Like most small birds, the European robin flies by "rowing" its way through the air. First, it pushes its wings down and back …

◀ … then it lifts its wings up for another stroke.

14

▼ Most of the muscles the robin uses to flap its wings are in its chest.

Some small birds are strong enough to fly across the ocean without stopping to rest.

▼ Birds steer with their tails while they push forward with their wings.

15

Hovering Hummingbird

Hummingbirds really do hum. They flap their wings so quickly (about 50 times a second) that they make a humming sound. Hummingbirds are unusual in many ways. They hover in front of flowers and use their long beaks to reach deep into the flowers for nectar. They can move their wings more than other birds, so they can hover in one place, fly up or down, or even fly backward. All that flying uses a lot of energy, so hummingbirds have to drink a lot of nectar to stay alive.

▼ In wintertime, the ruby-throated hummingbird flies 500 miles across the sea to find warm weather and nectar.

Some hummingbirds

Hummingbirds are the only birds that can fly backward.

▶ Sugar in nectar provides the energy hummingbirds need for hovering.

16

visit 2,000 flowers a day

▶ A hummingbird
flies forward by
flapping its wings
up and down …

▶ … and hovers
by flapping its
wings in a figure-
eight shape.

▶ To fly backward,
it flaps its wings
above and behind
its head.

17

A swan has powerful legs so it

Taking Off

All birds need air flowing over and under their wings before they can take off. A small, light bird such as a robin can make this happen just by jumping into the air. But big birds such as swans are hundreds of times heavier than robins. Before a swan can take off, it has to run along the water, like a plane gathering speed on a runway. Large birds also have very long wings that help them stay in the air for hours, or even days, at a time.

◄An albatross has long, narrow wings that help it glide across wide oceans, hunting fish and squid.

18

can run on water before taking off

▶ Flocks of geese fly
in a V-shape, taking
turns at the front.

◀ A swan needs a long
runway to take off, so it
must always land in a big
pond. If the pond was
too small, the swan would
not be able to fly away.

*The first bird
in a flock pushes
against the air and
makes it easier for
the other birds
to fly.*

19

Hunting on the Wing

Some birds hunt from the air. These birds of prey have superb eyesight, strong claws for catching food, and strong beaks for tearing flesh. Eagles and vultures have broad wings and soar for hours as they search the landscape below for prey. Some small birds of prey, such as falcons, have narrow wings and long tails. They need to twist and turn as they chase their prey through the air.

▲ One of the smallest birds of prey is the pygmy falcon. It hunts grasshoppers and other insects.

◄ Ospreys use their large, strong claws to clutch fish.

20

The peregrine falcon, a bird of prey, is the fastest thing on wings.

▼Vultures spend hours in the air looking for animals that are already dead. They tear flesh with their strong beaks.

▲A vulture uses its long wings to hitch a ride on a column of warm, rising air.

Wings Underwater

Penguins use their stiff wings, called flippers, to "fly" underwater as they hunt for fish, shrimp, and squid. They spend most of their lives in the sea, protected by a thick coat of feathers, and visit land only to lay eggs. Emperor penguins live in Antarctica, the coldest place on Earth. The ground is covered by ice, so they do not build nests. Instead, the fathers keep the eggs warm by carrying them on their feet. Every winter, thousands of emperor penguins huddle together for weeks without eating while they wait for their eggs to hatch.

Can you tell how the chinstrap penguin got its name?

▼ The fairy penguin is the tiniest of the 18 kinds of penguins. It is smaller than a chicken.

◀ Like other penguins, the rockhopper can dive to the dark depths of the ocean.

22

▼ The chinstrap penguin uses its long tail to balance itself on slippery ice.

▶ The emperor is the biggest penguin and is about four feet tall. It can survive colder weather than almost any other animal.

Flightless Wings

All birds have wings, but not all birds can fly. Ostriches and emus are too big to fly. When danger threatens, they can run away on their long, strong legs, or fight off attackers with the sharp claws on their toes. The kiwi, their relative, is about the size of a chicken. It sleeps during the day. At night, it searches the forest floor for earthworms with its long, slender bill. Most flightless birds lay big eggs, which hatch into big chicks. The chicks are able to run within a few hours of hatching.

▶ Father emus look after the eggs. When the chicks have hatched, he protects them from enemies and shows them what to eat.

◀ The kiwi's wings are so small that they are hidden beneath its feathers.

24

Ostrich and emu chicks are striped so they can hide in long grass.

An emu can run as fast as a horse can gallop

25

Furry Fliers

Bats are the only furry creatures that can truly fly. They have wings made of skin, which they can flap up and down. Bats fly at night, making very high sounds that bounce off the objects around them. They listen for the returning echoes to avoid bumping into things. Most bats are the size of a mouse or smaller, and feed on flying insects. Some bats feed on nectar, flowers, and fruit. Others catch frogs and fish. Vampire bats live on the blood of birds and animals.

▶ Some bats live together in caves. Thousands of them fly out at night to search for insects.

◀ Insect-eating bats find their food by bouncing sounds off moths and mosquitoes.

26

The bones in a bat's wings are actually very long hand bones.

◀ By spreading its long webbed fingers and toes, the flying frog can glide from one tree to another to escape an enemy.

Furry webs

Flying without Wings

Some forest animals glide from tree to tree to escape their enemies or to find food. These gliding frogs, snakes, lizards, squirrels, and possums do not have wings that they can flap up and down. Instead, they have webs of skin that act like parachutes and help them to fall slowly and safely. Flying frogs, lizards, and snakes can only glide for short distances of about 50 feet. Flying squirrels can glide for up to 150 feet. Some flying possums from Australia can glide for up to 200 feet.

Flying squirrels and flying possums can steer with their tails.

28

instead of wings

▲ Flying squirrels live
in the pine forests of
North America and
Asia. They glide from
one tree to another to
find nuts and insects.

Prehistoric Flight

▲ This pterosaur, called *Pteranodon,* had a long beak. It scooped up fish like a pelican does.

Pteranodon *could glide all day long. It hardly ever flapped its wings.*

Winged things have been on Earth for millions of years. Dragonflies and cockroaches, which are still around, appeared almost 100 million years before the dinosaurs. Flying reptiles, called pterosaurs, lived at the same time as the dinosaurs. The smallest pterosaur was the size of a crow, but the biggest was the size of a small plane. The earliest known bird was *Archaeopteryx*. Unlike birds today, it had teeth in its mouth and claws on its wings. It hunted insects and lizards.

▶ *Archaeopteryx* was about as big as a pigeon. Although it could fly, its wings were not very strong. It probably swooped on insects as they flew past its perch.

◀ Dragonflies have been on Earth for millions of years, but *Archaeopteryx* died out with the dinosaurs.

Other titles in the series:

ANIMAL BABIES
INCREDIBLE CREATURES
MIGHTY DINOSAURS
SCALY THINGS
UNDERWATER ANIMALS

Acknowledgments

(t=top, b=bottom, l=left, r=right, c=center, F=front cover, B=back cover)

Mike Atkinson/Garden Studio, 2, 24bl, 24/25, 32.
Christer Eriksson, 1, 6bl, 6/7c, 7tr, 30/31. **Helen Halliday/
Alex Lavroff & Associates,** 18l. **David Kirshner,** Ftl, 3tr, 4bl,
14tr, 14/15c, 18/19c, 19cr, 20bl, 22br, 23l, 23r, 28/29c, 30tl.
Frank Knight, 17r. **John Mac/Folio,** 12b, 13, 26b, 27c.
Robert Mancini, 4tl. **Tony Pyrzakowski,** 20tr, 20/21c.
Trevor Ruth, B, 3bl, 4/5c, 10b, 10/11c, 11tr, 16/17c.
Ray Sim, 9tr. **Kevin Stead,** Fc, 8/9c, 9b, 22bl, 28tl.